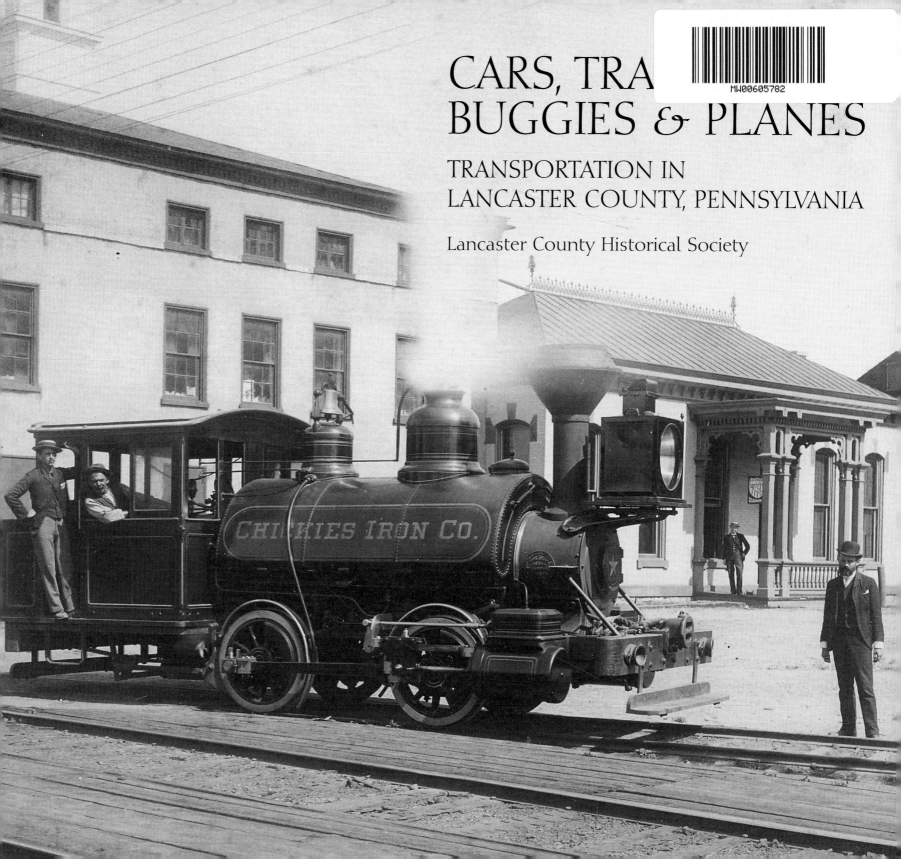

CARS, TRAINS, BUGGIES & PLANES

TRANSPORTATION IN LANCASTER COUNTY, PENNSYLVANIA

Lancaster County Historical Society

Acknowledgments

The Lancaster County Historical Society extends its thanks to Tamsin Wolff and Paul Herr of the Antique Automobile Club of America Museum for their assistance in identifying cars and trucks; Michael L. Abel, FLCHS, for his time and devotion to producing this volume; and volunteers Patricia B. Keene, Ph.D., and J. Roger Stemen for their years of dedication to the Photograph Collection.

Front cover: Harvey R. Williams sold and repaired bicycles and motorcycles on West Orange Street in 1915. LCHS D-12-04-65.
Previous page: Employees show off a locomotive engine (steam switcher) of the Chickies Iron Co., possibly at the Vesta Furnace in Marietta, circa 1890. LCHS 2-07-07-07.
Back cover (clockwise from top right): 1924 Model T truck, D-06-02-41; Mikado locomotive, circa 1927, D-06-05-44;
delivery wagon, 1903, 1-03-03-97; 1922 Ford Speedster, D-06-01-59; Harley-Davidson motorcycle and sidecar, 1929, A-09-02-78;
tri-motor aircraft, circa 1930, D-06-01-20; General Tire Company, 1931, D-06-04-80.

Project Manager: Marianne Heckles
Editors: James T. Alton; Thomas R. Ryan, Ph.D.
Design: Michael L. Abel, FLCHS
Printed by Cadmus Communications, Lancaster, Pennsylvania

ISBN 0-9740162-2-5
Library of Congress Control Number: 2005933481

Published by
Lancaster County Historical Society
230 North President Avenue, Lancaster, Pennsylvania 17603
www.lancasterhistory.org.

Contents

The Lancaster County Historical Society thanks the following businesses for their generous support of this book.

Presenting Sponsor

Supporting Sponsor

Foreword

All that we know of the world we know through the five senses. For most of us, our ability to see things is the most powerful tool we have for apprehending our surroundings. So what better way to approach the past than through the images created through the photographer's gaze and the camera's eye?

As historians we seek to understand the past by asking questions about it. In our quest for understanding we usually turn to documents, such as letters, diaries, or civil records, to test our hypotheses and refine our arguments. Less frequently we turn to objects—a chair, a teacup, or a building—and attempt to mine them for clues about the maker, seller, buyer, user, or even better, the community at large. From these bits and pieces of the past we assemble what we hope are meaningful stories about people in the past.

Historical societies are the repositories of these bits and pieces of the past. One of the most illuminating portals to days gone by can be found in the wonderful collections of photographic images in our care. Unfortunately, these collections are often inaccessible, poorly cared for, or just too low on the institutional list of priorities. Yet, thanks to the painstaking work of several volunteers, benefactors, foundations, and the wonders of modern technology, all of the Lancaster County Historical Society's photos are catalogued and readily available for your viewing. Our goal is to share this remarkable resource with you.

Entering its 120th year the Lancaster County Historical Society is a historical society in the classical sense of the term: one part history research library (published works and associated resources), one part manuscript collection (letters, diaries, government records), and one part artifact assemblage. Somewhere in the midst of these books, papers, and objects resides a collection of more than 13,000 photographs that seems at one moment to fit into all three categories, and the next moment, to fit into none of them at all.

Photographs have a unique immediacy that sets them apart as historical resources. Often they are the only record of an event to survive to the present. They introduce us to people, objects, events, and moments in ways that are almost real-time. We become bystanders viewing the past almost as it happened. We look at old photos and can imagine our forebears walking into the picture, even glancing back at us with a tip of the hat. Streetscapes seem to hum with the bustle of trolleys and cars. Smokestacks on factories evoke the clamor of heavy machinery and the work of many hands. Products on store shelves look ripe for the picking. These truly are windows into parts of the past.

With this volume on transportation in Lancaster County, we offer you a glimpse of the Lancaster County Historical Society's extensive photograph collection. This rich resource of more than 13,000 images is available for your perusal with the click of a mouse at our headquarters on the corner of North President and Marietta Avenues in Lancaster, Pennsylvania. You may even arrange for affordable reproductions of any of our photographs. Come take a look—you may be surprised by who or what you find!

Our photo collection continues to grow, too, through new acquisitions. In fact, one of the largest portions of our photographic collection was a donation from the Darmstaetter Photo Supply Company, formerly located at 37 North Queen Street in Lancaster. Darmstaetter's served Lancaster from about 1905 until 1976. The photo collection offers images from circa 1910 through the early 1940s and is a wonderful tool for interpreting twentieth-century Lancaster County history.

Perhaps you have old photos that depict some aspect of life in Lancaster County that you would like to share with others. With a firm commitment to chronicling the history of the twentieth century, we are particularly interested in receiving photos depicting life in Lancaster County from the recent past. If you would like to add your images to this important historical collection for present and future generations of inquiring Lancastrians, please contact us and let us know (717-392-4633). Even if you are not prepared to part with the original, in this digital age we will be honored to make a copy for our collection.

Thank you for joining us on this photographic foray into Lancaster County's past. Please stay tuned for future volumes in this series.

Thomas R. Ryan, Ph.D.
Executive Director
Lancaster County Historical Society

Introduction

Thomas R. Winpenny, Ph.D.

L ife is pretty simple. Everyone needs food, clothing, and shelter. To get this, most people have to work. To have jobs you first have to have a viable economy. As a county or nation grows, this economy needs to grow. Historically, a growing transportation network has generally been a prerequisite for a burgeoning economy. Scholars such as George Rogers Taylor and Walt Rostow have spilled a lot of ink demonstrating the connection between new modes of transportation and self-sustaining economic growth, particularly in the nineteenth century and particularly with the influence of the railroad.

HORSES

The much-beloved and storied horse was really a mixed blessing in the American past. There is no question concerning the critical role this animal played. Early political leaders rode about the countryside visiting their constituents and hoping to make a magnificent presentation of themselves sitting atop a beautiful animal. It surely worked for George Washington. Methodist ministers became the now-famous "circuit riders" by using horses to serve multiple churches on a single day. The equally famous Pony Express delivered the U.S. Mail through dangerous territory with heroic riders outracing Indians (as they were known in the nineteenth century). Countless farmers used horses for plowing. And, of course, these animals pulled wagons laden with goods well into the twentieth century. Socially, people rode for pleasure and the life of a country gentleman was associated, inextricably, with the horse. With all these positive contributions, how could anyone contend that the horse was a mixed blessing?

Consider the other side of the story. Horses required a great deal of care, housing, brushing, feeding, shoeing, and medical attention. A broken leg meant the end of a horse. The animals were easily frightened on the streets of nineteenth-century Lancaster by loud noises, and the newspapers contain endless stories of horses that got scared, reared up, bolted, and ran down the street and ultimately smashed through a plate glass window. This was a terrifying sight! The animals

Annie E. Stephan of Elizabethtown continued the family produce business after the death of her husband, Charles. Here, Annie stands with a basket of goods in front of the family's produce wagon, circa 1910. LCHS 1-02-03-74.

1

also left quite a mess on the streets, and Professor Joel Tarr of Carnegie Mellon University has even calculated the tonnage for Pittsburgh for those with a need to know. Most important, however, on the negative side of the ledger, horse and wagon transportation was never very efficient. Furthermore, the efficiency could not be improved very much with better technology, the way a canal or railroad might. The horse and wagon represented slow, sluggish, and inefficient transport. Ironically, in the modern age we are "rediscovering" the horse. Mounted police have returned to many cities, and our spirits were lifted during the Great Depression of the 1930s by the heroics of Seabiscuit and more recently in 2004 by Smarty Jones!

TRAINS

After the horse we sometimes think of the "iron horse" or "ferroequinology" as one clever person put it. As you may recall the railroad almost bypassed Lancaster, and that would have been a disaster for the local economy. But the train did finally come to town in the 1830s, right through the downtown, and it was a hazard. The sparks that flew were dangerous, the whistles that blew were annoying, and the locomotives kept running over and killing both citizens and livestock. Yes, it's hard to believe that people couldn't get out of the way of locomotives, but many did not and more than a few drunks who wandered onto the tracks were quickly dispatched to their "heavenly reward." Unlike the horse, the railroad represented a new technology that could be improved endlessly—and it was. For this reason the iron horse went on to become what historian John Stover at Purdue University called the single most important historical fact of the nineteenth century.

A train hurries across the Pennsylvania Railroad bridge over the Conestoga River on its way into the city of Lancaster. One of the bridge's archways frames the Lancaster Waterworks building. LCHS 1-01-04-72.

In Lancaster, of course, the train tracks were ultimately moved to the northern end of town and that made it safer for all. (It was never easy to tell the Pennsylvania Railroad what to do.) Over time numerous improvements came: more comfortable coaches, even metal coaches that wouldn't catch fire in an accident; Westinghouse air braking systems; better and safer coupling devices; better signals; and better timing and accurate schedule keeping thanks to Lancaster's Hamilton Watch, known worldwide as "The Watch of Railroad Accuracy." There is almost no limit to how much could be done to improve the modern iron horse. One of the more significant developments in the twentieth century is the extent to which the railroad has allowed Lancaster to become a bedroom community of Philadelphia—or is it the other way round? The terribly influential railroad, alas, lost

most or all of its growth potential after 1920 when, at least for Americans, it appeared to be superceded by the automobile, bus, and motor truck. (The bankruptcy of the Penn-Central Railroad in the 1970s was an exercise in "thinking the unthinkable.")

BICYCLES

The bicycle craze of the 1890s, by definition, took the country by storm. Perhaps the great Two Wheelers helped Lancastrians and others take their minds off the economic depression of the decade. Between 1893 and 1898 the country went through what was, up to that point in history, the most serious economic downturn we had ever witnessed, punctuated by staggering unemployment and labor violence. Interest in bicycles seems to move in fits and starts—surely the

automobile put a damper on the craze of the 1890s. Throughout the twentieth century the nation never seemed to become as enamored with bikes as the Europeans, possibly explained by our relatively cheap fuel.

A young man enjoys a bicycle ride in the country around Christiana in 1930. LCHS D-05-02-71.

TROLLEYS

Trolleys played a major role in nineteenth- and twentieth-century urban-American life, but most thoughtful people believe their role should have been even larger and should have been maintained forever. Trolley tracks covered Lancaster County as spokes coming out of the hub of a wheel, with the city of Lancaster serving as the hub. There is an article in the *Journal of the Lancaster County Historical Society* with maps that depict the golden age of trolleys. This mode of transportation

Penn Square, encircled with trolleys during the 1920s. The six-story building to the right of the elaborate old Woolworth Building was the short-lived Examiner Building. It was demolished in 1928 to make way for a new Fulton Bank building. LCHS 2-07-07-06.

was both cheap and efficient. But note that the trolley was a broad solution to the transportation issue, a community solution. In many ways it could never hope to compete with the automobile that offered more freedom and a sense of individualism. Nothing was more frustrating to the red-blooded American motorist than to be stuck behind a slow-moving trolley that he could not pass. The only solution, believe it or not, was to get rid of trolleys altogether. Of course, the American auto industry worked hard to bury trolleys—some would contend, including scholars, that there was even a major *conspiracy* in Detroit to do so. To be sure, a trolley ride is still the best way to tour a city such as New Orleans, but to many they are simply un-American.

As a fascinating footnote to history, in 1948 there was a major trolley strike in Philadelphia over the question of whether Negroes should be permitted to be motormen and drive the trolleys. (The last trolleys disappeared from the streets of Philadelphia, on Germantown Avenue, about 1991. They are occasionally brought back for historic tours.) Lancaster County has managed to eliminate both trolleys and trolley tracks, with only a rubber-tired "motorized" trolley currently in use.

AIRCRAFT

Aviation is another area covered by this book, and perhaps many Lancastrians do not know that a very famous hot air balloonist, John Wise, was a local celebrity. Wise was not only a great pioneer balloonist in the nineteenth century, but he also gained scientific recognition for his study of west-to-east wind currents. The Smithsonian is quite aware of John Wise and his research and holds him in high regard.

Because of the eternal limitations of hot air ballooning, such as unpredictable travel routes, many turned their attention to fixed-wing aircraft, pioneered at the turn of the century by the Wright brothers at Kitty Hawk, North Carolina. The Red Rose City was in the vanguard of interest in fixed-wing aircraft not only for sport but for practical business purposes. Lancaster became one of the early cities in the commonwealth to have its own airport, and over time it became more and more sophisticated in its equipment and practices. Other airports have since grown up around the county, including the increasingly famous Smoketown Airport. Air travel exploded across America in the twentieth century, and ultimately the Lancaster Airport offered regularly scheduled flights. Ironically, in recent years the hot air balloonists have made a major comeback in the area, and many people give balloon rides today as birthday gifts. A good history of local aviation (fixed-wing aircraft) has been produced by William Krantz for the *Journal of the Lancaster County Historical Society*.

BOATS

Boats of all sorts have been part of local history, but obviously much of the county has been excluded by reason of geography. The towns of Columbia and Marietta, by contrast, owe their prominence to their location on the Susquehanna River. Through much of the nineteenth century, lumber and other commodities made their way from north-central Pennsylvania down the Susquehanna River to Columbia and Marietta for resale and distribution to areas as distant as Philadelphia and Baltimore. These river towns flourished in a fashion that we can only imagine today. Other uses for watercraft included a modest canal in the nineteenth century headed south from the city of Lancaster, and some boating on the Conestoga, where only locals can convince themselves that it is a "river." Today citizens take their power boats and sail craft to the Susquehanna for pleasure outings, but many countians remain rather distant from water. Much history surrounds the several Columbia–Wrightsville bridges, and they can be researched at the Lancaster County Historical Society or the Columbia Historical Society.

The Evelyn B. *makes its way along the Conestoga River on a sunny summer afternoon during the early 1900s. It was among the fleet of paddleboats that included the famous* Lady Gay. *LCHS 1-03-04-19.*

AUTOMOBILES

Few things in American history compare with the automobile revolution, something that several scholars have devoted a lifetime to studying. What is easily forgotten is that in the early part of the twentieth century there were literally hundreds of automobile builders, with most concentrated in New England and the mid-Atlantic States. They could be found dotting the maps of York, Berks, and Lancaster Counties. (The famous name *Fleetwood* came from a town by the same name in Berks County.) These were well-established shops that had a history of building vehicles such as carriages, wagons, or bicycles, and thus they had already wrestled with some of the issues concerning

5

locomotion, speed, steering, braking, and the like. It was not a great leap for these shops to make a transition to automobiles.

Sometimes we forget that steam-powered and electric-powered cars were quite popular and the technology was surely workable and viable in the early 1900s. Indeed, Oliver Evans had a steam-powered "automobile"—actually a dredger—on the streets of Philadelphia as early as 1806. It is only with hindsight that we know that the internal combustion engine became the final solution for much of the twentieth century, or at least until recently. (Incidentally, aircraft were utilizing the same basic engine.) Gasoline in that golden era of the early auto sold for a few cents per gallon and not $3.00. The Pennsylvania Railroad, which controlled the state legislature, did everything in its power to block the construction of highways, arguing it was most unfair for one mode to have to build its own tracks and right-of-way and a newer mode have its highways built by the government. Today, the state has more miles of highway than any other state. Pennsylvania may also lead the nation in deteriorating highways, unsafe and dangerous bridges, and potholes.

One of the unique outcomes of the automotive revolution has been to turn Lancaster County into a tourist mecca. Starting with the Broadway play *Plain and Fancy* in the 1950s and

Floor shows, such as this one at Chambers Motor Co., were a way for people to see the latest makes and models. In this case, the latest Buicks in 1926 were on display at the Chambers showroom at North Prince and West Orange Streets in Lancaster. LCHS D-06-03-44.

continuing through the film *Witness* to the 1990s, the Amish have been heralded as a group of quaint religious primitives (anti-technologists) that city folk just have to see. With the use of the car, forty million potential tourists are only a two-hour drive away in Philadelphia, New York, Washington, and Baltimore. Accordingly, a vast tourist industry has grown up—from motels to restaurants to gift shops to gas stations—serving at least 5 million tourists each year, primarily during the warmer months.

Yet another way to look at this is to see that the automotive revolution produced not only tourists, but many who decided to move permanently to Lancaster. In 2005 the county has almost 500,000 citizens and continues to grow rapidly. Furthermore, it has become a retirement haven as well with the greatest concentration and number of retirees outside of Florida. (Pennsylvania does not tax retirement income.) In sum, of the many who came to visit Amish Country by auto, quite a few decided to move here and many decided to retire here.

SERVICE STATIONS

Gas and service stations are both symbols and reminders that you can't have an automotive revolution without dramatically altering the landscape. And so the car brought not only the questionably attractive stations but other visual delights, such as motels (Remember what the early ones looked like?), drive-in restaurants, drive-in movie theaters, and ultimately multistory parking garages.

The gas and service stations required thousands of mechanics to maintain and service the autos. It is rumored that good mechanics have always been in short supply. Furthermore, America's love affair with the auto meant that (perhaps unconsciously) the national rail network was permitted to deteriorate. With declining interest in rail transportation, the U.S. Congress in the Eisenhower years of the 1950s turned to funding an interstate highway network that seemed to be very much in keeping with the wishes of the American people.

Those wanting super service could stop by Frick's Super Service Station and Greasing Palace on East Liberty Street for a royal tune-up and a tank of Sinclair gasoline. LCHS D-06-04-33.

TRUCKS

The motor truck helped to further bury the railroad by cutting into freight once carried by rail. This does not mean that trucks started to haul coal or grain in any significant way, but they did carry a lot of l.c.l. (less than carload) freight. Trucks also contributed to the decentralization of urban industry and the growth of suburban industrial parks, but that is another story for another day.

The advent of the truck also led to a great debate over whether the horse and wagon or truck was the better vehicle for the twentieth-century businessman. Anyone might be surprised by the length and intensity of this discussion, but in the end the motor truck won out. Why? Because they were an attractive novelty and because a few new trucks or a fleet of new trucks said to your customers that your business was both modern and successful. In the early decades of the twentieth century most businesses did not want to be seen as "horse and buggy" operations. Of course, motor trucks were built in Lancaster, and the Lancaster County Historical Society has an abundance of material on the subject, including a few *Journal* articles and a book.

Perhaps the most spectacular trucks this author is aware of (from this early period) were owned by the Curtis Publishing Company of Philadelphia, publishers of *The Saturday Evening Post, Ladies Home*

Philip F. Fellman, roofer and sheet metal worker, applied for a patent for the contraption he hauled around in the back of his 1924 Ford Model T truck. The patent-pending machinery may have been used to heat tar for Fellman's roofing business, which he operated at the corner of South Dorwart and Lafayette Streets in Lancaster. LCHS D-06-02-41.

Journal, and *Holiday* magazines. These magnificent vehicles were large stake trucks with a flat bed, painted forest green with gold lettering. These electric trucks were powered by batteries that required frequent recharging. The solid rubber tires made for a rough ride over the cobblestone streets of Center City Philadelphia. The burly drivers appeared to be draped over two "steering wheels." Actually, the top wheel was a steering wheel and the wheel below it was used to shift gears. (The author actually worked on these trucks as an 18 year old.) These cumbersome vehicles were used to transfer huge rolls of paper for the printing presses from the Philadelphia plant at 6th and Sansom Streets (across the street from Independence Hall) to the presses at the Sharon Hill plant, just west of the city. These trucks were on the streets as late as the 1960s, even though they were not equipped to run at high speeds on roads such as the Pennsylvania Turnpike. There were few better ads than these unusual trucks lumbering around the urban landscape. The Red Rose City had early electric trucks as well that belonged to the Herr Ice Company. According to Richard Herr, grandson of the owner, the trucks were brought in from New York state and sported two large Exide batteries on each side. One of the Herr Ice trucks is in the collection of the Landis Valley Farm Museum. Electrics never really became a big success as either commercial or leisure vehicles, with the exception of several million golf carts that are sometimes overlooked.

Incredibly, though some of these modes of transport have seen their day or been relegated to novelty status in most of America, Lancaster County still embraces all in one form or another. Horse-drawn buggies and wagons provide transportation for passengers and freight and mules do the work of tractors. (The clip-clop of hooves and the racket of steel wheels on pavement can even be heard in Lancaster City.) The simple two-wheeler has been elevated to a higher plane with an annual cycling "Grand Prix" through city streets. The short rail ride from Strasburg to Paradise is meant to be an attraction rather than transportation in the truest sense, but these trains are housed in the premier tribute to steam locomotion in the United States.

In a little over three centuries, Lancaster County has grown through and along with the advances in transportation. In this book we pay tribute to all the ways we got from here to there.

SELECTED BIBLIOGRAPHY

George Rogers Taylor, *The Transportation Revolution, 1815–1860 (Economic History of the United States, Vol. 4)*. M.E. Sharpe, Inc., January 1977.

Walt Rostow, *The Stages of Economic Growth: A Non-Communist Manifesto*. Cambridge University Press, 1991.

Joel Tarr, *The Search for the Ultimate Sink: Urban Pollution in Historical Perspective (Series on Technology and the Environment)*. University of Akron Press, Akron, Ohio, 1996.

John Stover, *History of the Baltimore and Ohio Railroad*. Purdue University Press, 1987.

Gary R. Hovenin, "Lancaster's Streetcar Suburbs, 1890–1920," *Journal of the Lancaster County Historical Society*, Vol. 82, No. 1, 1978, pp. 48–59.

William E. Krantz, "A History of Aeronautics in Lancaster County, PA," *Journal of the Lancaster County Historical Society*, Vol. 90, No. 3, 1986, pp. 118–189.

Donald J. Summar, "History of the Kreider Machine Company," *Journal of the Lancaster County Historical Society*, Vol. 76, No. 1, 1972, pp. 41–44.

Donald J. Summar, "Carroll Motor Car Company of Strasburg," *Journal of the Lancaster County Historical Society*, Vol. 77, No. 3, 1973, pp. 133–142.

Donald J. Summar, "Rowe Motor History: 1908–1925," *Journal of the Lancaster County Historical Society*, Vol. 79, No. 2, 1979, pp. 43–130.

Donald J. Summar, "A History of the Conestoga Motor Truck Company," *Journal of the Lancaster County Historical Society*, Vol. 73, No. 4, 1969, pp. 210–217.

Donald J. Summar, "The Thomas Wagon Company of Lititz: Pioneer Motor Truck Manufacturer in Lancaster County," *Journal of the Lancaster County Historical Society*, Vol. 79, No. 1, 1975, pp. 15–22.

Pilot Jesse Jones stands with R.L. Gerhart Company's Ryan monoplane, which advertised El Capitan Coffee. This is thought to be the first business aircraft purchased by a Lancaster County company. It was the sister ship of the Ryan "Spirit of St. Louis" flown by Charles Lindburgh from New York to Paris in May, 1927. LCHS 2-08-05-49.

Horsing Around

Marianne Heckles

For thousands of years, people have relied on the trusty horse to haul around their goods and chattels, not to mention themselves. Early horsepower was not just a means of getting from one place to another. It contributed mightily to trade and commerce.

The history of Lancaster County cannot be told without mentioning the Conestoga wagon. Some folks considered them the forefather of the prairie schooners of the West, whereas others called them "ships of inland commerce." Historically speaking, these wagons were the precursor to the moving van, the utility truck, and the big rig. Whether schlepping coal from mine to port or moving a family to a new homestead, the Conestoga wagon was a major player in the early American way of life.

In the early twentieth century, many local businesses used horses and wagons to transport a variety of goods to their customers. Patrons didn't even have to go to market. A horse, cart, and driver could bring milk, bread, vegetables, or meat right to your front door.

As a mode of transportation, the horse and buggy is not outdated, at least in Lancaster County. Travel any back road in the county and you're bound to come across an Amish family going from one place to the next. It's just further proof that no matter how much things seem to change in our society, some things still stay the same.

Left: At the beginning of the twentieth century, Lancaster City contracted with Norris D. Alexander to sprinkle the city's dusty streets. In this 1905 photo, Alexander drives his horse team and water tank along West James Street past Lancaster Theological Seminary. LCHS 3-06-01-05.

Above: Christopher Hager opened his dry goods store on West King Street in 1821. In 1909 (photo), horse-drawn wagons delivered merchandise for the store, then operated by brothers Walter C. and William H. Hager. By the 1950s, Hager's had become America's oldest department store continuously operated at the same site. The store served generations of Lancastrians before closing its doors in 1977. LCHS 2-06-01-24.

Daniel S. Bursk and his son, J. Howard Bursk, were in the grocery business in Lancaster from the 1860s to the 1910s. Their delivery wagon hauled goods from their store at 17 East King Street to their patrons. LCHS 1-01-03-27.

Even as late as 1953, Queen Dairy delivered milk to its patrons with a horse-drawn wagon. LCHS A-08-01-15.

A young lady takes her horse and open carriage on an excursion through the city, circa 1914. The Western Union Telegraph and Cable Office in the background occupied the northeast corner of Penn Square from the early 1880s to 1925. LCHS 2-03-07-38.

An unidentified salesman stands with the Schlotzhauer Saxon Bakery wagon, circa 1920. The wagon advertised bread, rolls, and fancy cakes. LCHS A-09-02-40.

Horse processions and shows were quite popular at the turn of the twentieth century. Clubs, such as the Road Drivers Association, held meets to show off their well-trained horses. At left, White Socks and High Socks exhibit grand style for the crowd. LCHS D-02-04-33. Below left: White Socks, owned by George W. Swain, performs at a circa 1919 horse show. LCHS D-02-04-29.

Opposite: Perhaps named for the region of its origin, the Conestoga wagon was considered the workhorse of transportation vehicles in its day. Popular from the early 1700s to the mid-1800s, the wagon helped move America westward. LCHS 2-04-04-30.

Horses haul a wagon precariously loaded with chairs from the Hoffmeier Brothers Furniture Store on the first block of East King Street in Lancaster. Hoffmeier's served Lancaster from about 1865 to 1935. The photograph was probably taken between 1900 and 1910. LCHS D-11-01-75.

Driver David Huss brought the finest Kunzler meats to customers with his horse and beautifully decorated wagon. The photo was taken about 1903. LCHS 1-03-03-67.

All Aboard

John Ward Willson Loose, FLCHS

The 1834 arrival of the Columbia to Philadelphia Railroad heralded the beginning of train service in Lancaster County. When the Pennsylvania Railroad bought the State Works in 1857, the "Pennsy" began extending its lines throughout Lancaster County and beyond. It began by leasing lines connecting Lancaster with Harrisburg. In the 1870s, the Columbia and Port Deposit Railroad linked Lancaster with the main Philadelphia–Baltimore–Washington line. Other branches from the Pennsy's main line extended from Lancaster to New Holland, Narvon, Honeybrook, and Downingtown.

continued…

Above: The Columbia and Reading Railroad locomotive "Robert Crane," built in 1864 by Norris Locomotive Works in Lancaster. It later became Philadelphia and Reading No. 1088 before it was scrapped in 1897. LCHS 1-01-03-63.

Left: A group of men stand next to a Mikado locomotive, circa 1927. This particular train was hauling salt. LCHS D-06-05-44.

Increased freight traffic on the Pennsylvania Railroad led to the construction of a bypass around Lancaster from Dillerville to a point just east of Lancaster City. Only local trains traveled the main line through downtown. The eastern junction of the main line and the bypass was located near the former RCA plant southeast of New Holland Avenue. If engineers or controllers fell asleep at the switch, trains could and did collide at this spot. The famous "Kidney Wreck" of 1919 occurred here.

Other early railroad lines included the "Little, Old, and Slow" narrow-gauge track that ran across the southern end of Lancaster County from Peach Bottom to Oxford, Chester County. Another early line connected the Pennsy main line at Leamon Place to Strasburg. The Strasburg Railroad and its old-fashioned steam locomotive continue to attract tourists to Lancaster County today.

Passengers await the arrival of the next train at the Pennsylvania Railroad Station in New Holland. This photograph was taken about 1890. LCHS 2-04-01-19.

Pennsylvania Railroad workers pose in front of Engine No. 152 in Lancaster, circa 1890. LCHS 1-01-04-08.

In April 1912, President Theodore Roosevelt made a campaign stop in Lancaster. He addressed a large crowd from the balcony of the Caldwell House, the hotel to the left of the train in the photograph. The Hotel Brunswick now occupies the corner of Queen and Chestnut where Roosevelt spoke. LCHS 1-02-02-08.

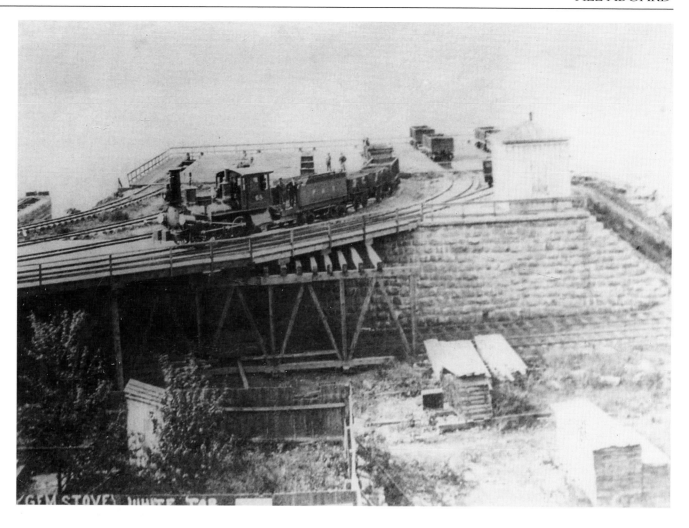

The Reading and Columbia Railroad opened in 1864 and was at the height of its operations when this photograph of Engine No. 68 was taken, circa 1880. It shows the coal loading wharf on the canal in Columbia. The railroad made stops at both the Chickies and Mt. Hope iron furnaces. LCHS 1-01-04-15.

A group of men poses with Philadelphia and Reading's No. 1090 at the engine house in Columbia, circa 1890. This engine, built by Lancaster's Norris Locomotive Works, had previously been called the "Ephrata" when it operated as part of the Reading and Columbia Railroad. LCHS 1-03-03-72.

In 1929 the Pennsylvania Railroad's new station replaced an eyesore of a building at Queen and Chestnut Streets. Its new location moved train service a mile north, out of downtown, to northern Lancaster City. The McGovern Avenue station continues to serve passengers, now as a stop for AMTRAK trains running between Harrisburg and Philadelphia. LCHS 1-01-03-22.

Locals called the Lancaster, Oxford, and Southern Railway the "Little, Old, and Slow." This narrow-gauge line provided service between the Quarryville station, pictured above, and Oxford, in Chester County, until 1914. LCHS 1-04-01-67.

A lone locomotive sits on the tracks at the Dillerville train station, located at the current site of Armstrong World Industries along Dillerville Road. The photograph was taken about 1895. LCHS 1-01-03-38.

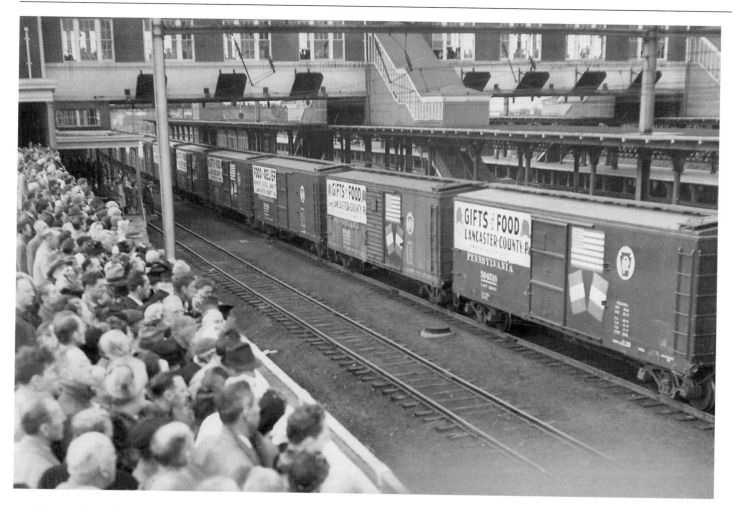

Thousands watch Lancaster County's Gifts of Food to the Friendship Food Train roll away from the station during the winter of 1948–1949. The local contribution was part of a nationwide effort to help feed the hungry of Europe after World War II. LCHS A-09-01-06.

The Pennsylvania Railroad's new Lancaster station on McGovern Avenue awaits its first passengers, circa 1929. The station paved the way for development in the northern part of Lancaster City. LCHS D-13-03-54.

The Great Wreck of April 21, 1896, occurred during a heavy storm when an unattended boxcar started blowing down the tracks from a siding at White Oak in Penn Township. The boxcar gathered momentum as it rolled downhill, eventually colliding with the "night buck" freight train as it approached Manheim from Reading, killing the freight train's brakeman. LCHS 2-06-06-07.

Lancaster's worst train wreck happened on the foggy morning of November 17, 1919, at what is now the site of RCA and McCaskey High School. At a railway intersection southeast of New Holland Avenue, the Buffalo Flyer passenger train sideswiped a freight train hauling frozen meat products. The crash injured six passengers on the Flyer and killed the freight train's engineer and brakeman. "The Kidney Wreck," as it is now known, spilled frozen meat across the nearby fields, providing a feast for neighborhood dogs for days. LCHS D-07-03-17.

To serve its patrons in Lancaster, the Pennsylvania Railroad built a station in 1860 at the corner of North Queen and East Chestnut Streets. During its heyday, the station was a bustling hub of trade and traffic, complete with newsstands and restaurants. By the 1920s the aging station has become an eyesore. The Lancaster Chamber of Commerce hung a large banner across North Queen Street, apologizing "Don't Judge Our City by Its Station." A new station, constructed on McGovern Avenue in the northern part of the city in 1929, serves travelers to this day.

Left: A horse and wagon and an electric trolley car symbolize an era just before the advent of the automobile. The train station at Queen and Chestnut Streets was still a busy depot, and personal transportation remained an idea for the future. LCHS 2-06-09-25.

Top right: The downtown train station during busier times, circa 1890. The street light protruding from the building at left belonged to the Globe Hotel. The Globe closed its doors in 1929. LCHS 2-06-06-03.

Right: A train makes its way into the old station at Chestnut and Queen during the 1920s. Note the newly constructed Hotel Brunswick to the left of the station. LCHS 2-06-06-05.

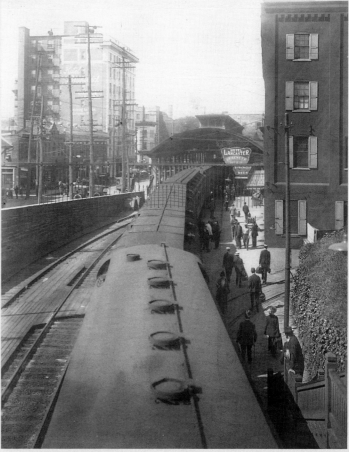

Above: Taken from Chestnut Street in 1929, this photograph shows the demolition of the old train station in the city of Lancaster. The Globe Hotel had already been torn down. The building to left of the photograph on the south side of Chestnut street is now the site of the Armstrong showroom building. LCHS 2-06-06-25.

Left: The sign above the group of men warns pedestrians, "Railroad Crossing, STOP, Look and Listen." The image shows the old station in its final days in 1929. LCHS 2-06-09-32.

Two Wheelers

Barry R. Rauhauser

John Wise, Lancaster's nineteenth-century extreme sports athlete, may have been the area's first bicyclist when he crafted a 60-pound bicycle out of wood and iron in the 1860s. The heavy, slow, bone-shaking device he built, however, did not catch on until the next decade, when enlarged front wheels provided better gearing and pneumatic tires offered a more forgiving ride. The bicycle assumed its most recognizable form by 1885, as inventors replaced the dangerous mismatched wheel sizes of the high-wheeler with the same-sized wheels of the chain-driven safety bicycle. The bicycle craze had begun, and by 1900 more than a million bicycles had been produced in America.

The Marietta Bicycle Club formed in the early 1880s and was followed only a few years later by the Lancaster Wheelmen. The clubs brought together bicycle enthusiasts for the occasional "run" to villages in the county. A bicycle school opened on North Queen Street, bicycle stunt shows were held at McGrann's Park, and the 1896 Thanksgiving Day parade featured seven large groups of bicycle riders from around the county.

The result of the bicycle's immense popularity at the end of the nineteenth century can be seen every day in the ribbons of asphalt that crisscross the nation. Lancaster's many bicycle clubs joined the League of American Wheelmen, which worked to improve the nation's wagon-rutted roads and lobbied for the creation of a federal road department.

The history of the motorcycle paralleled the evolution of the bicycle. As early as 1867 inventors attempted to take the leg work out of bike riding by attaching engines of various sorts. Within thirty years, production motor-powered bicycles impressed the world with their economy, power, and reliability. In 1903, William Harley and Arthur Davidson, a pair of Midwestern kids in their twenties, got their first bike

continued…

Left: Six gentlemen pause for a photograph before setting off on a ride near Terre Hill, sometime between 1890 and 1900. LCHS 2-08-01-07.

Above: Young Charles Longenecker proudly poses with his bike, circa 1890. LCHS 1-05-02-09.

to rumble to life, making American motorcycle history.

In Lancaster, the motorcycle caught on quickly, with dealers and mechanics in business as early as 1910. Many, like Harvey Williams, were already tinkering with and repairing bicycles. Williams, the first to sell Indian motorcycles in Lancaster, opened up shop on Lancaster Avenue, between Frederick and James Streets, but soon moved to West Orange Street. "Harwilco" was quite popular with the cycling crowd until the business closed its doors in 1990.

Other bike dealers and mechanics in Lancaster included the Flory brothers, Jacob and Daniel, who operated a shop at 161 East King Street during the 1910s and 1920s. They made repairs and sold parts and gasoline. They were the area's first purveyors of Pope motorcycles.

Behind his home near Landisville, Raymond Franklin Bitner rides a bicycle built by John Wise. The fifteen-year-old lad was riding an antique, as the photograph was taken around 1915, about fifty years after Wise built the 60-pound machine. The bicycle is now part of the collections of the Lancaster County Historical Society. LCHS 1-04-01-02.

A man rests with his bike along a city street in this photograph, taken circa 1900. LCHS D-05-01-06.

Howard Dorsey and brothers Martin and William Caulfield prepare to set off for a bike hike in the early 1920s. They departed from the Dorseys' backyard at 136 East Lemon Street in Lancaster. LCHS A-09-02-62.

Right: "Parts for all makes of machines," advertised Harvey R. Williams. A former racer of motorcycles and bicycles, Williams was in the repair business as early as 1910. He operated this shop at 626–628 West Orange Street until his death in 1940. LCHS D-12-04-65.

Conestoga Publishing Company, established in 1906, made its delivery service speedier in the 1920s with the addition of a Harley-Davidson motorcycle and sidecar. LCHS A-09-02-78.

Pictured with their Harley-Davidsons are Lancaster's first motorcycle policemen (from left), Harry Resh and David N. Trapnell. They zoomed into action on Lancaster's city streets in 1911. LCHS 1-04-01-16.

Motorcycles first entered military service during World War I. Doughboys loved the speedy and rebellious allure of the bikes and put them to good civilian use at home after the war. Photos of young soldiers on their powerful new machines made their way back to Lancaster, where anxious families waited to see what developed at the Darmstaetter Photo Supply Co. Here, an unidentified soldier sits on his Harley-Davidson. LCHS D-04-02-70.

A young John Dickel of 710 East End Avenue in Lancaster and two friends squeeze onto a motorcycle and sidecar sometime during 1921. LCHS D-07-01-10.

Another doughboy, possibly Sgt. Ray S. Hendricks of Mountville, poses with a motorcycle. LCHS D-04-03-41.

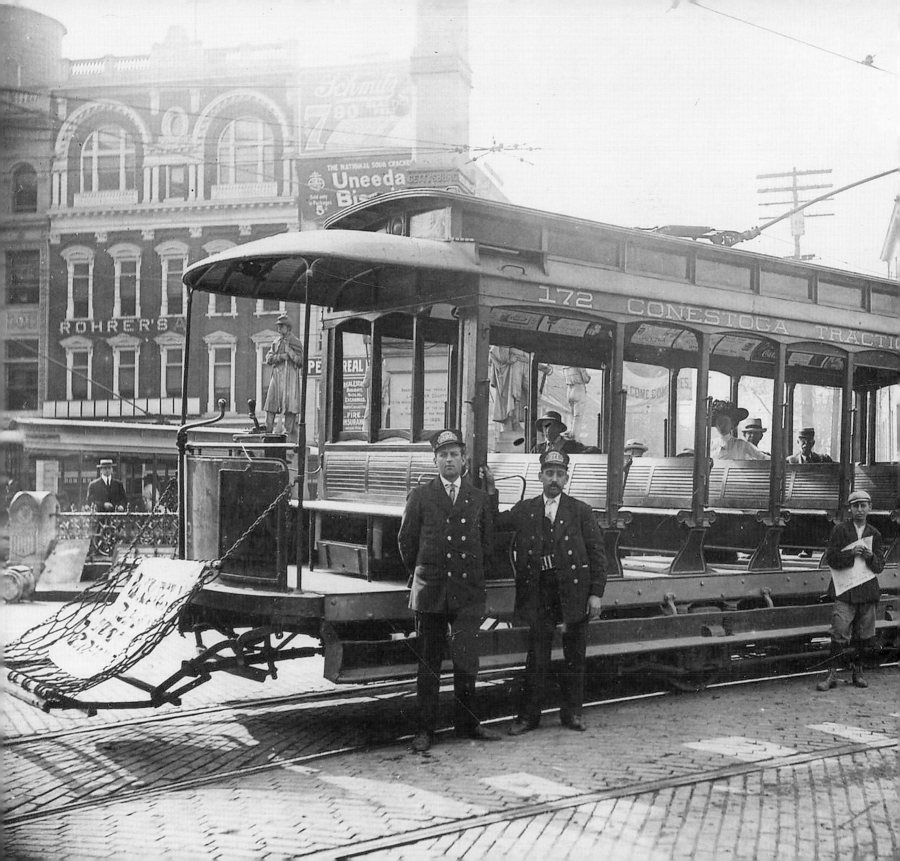

Clang, Clang, Clang

John Ward Willson Loose, FLCHS

Long distance travel at the turn of the nineteenth century usually meant a ride on the railroad, but a short jaunt from Lancaster to Lititz required only a ride on a trolley car. Lancaster County's first trolley lines were horse-drawn cars. In the 1870s they carried passengers to such destinations as Millersville State Normal School, Maple Grove on the west end of Lancaster, and McGrann's Park on the east end. In the 1880s trolley or streetcar lines expanded east out New Holland Avenue and East King Street. By 1890, most lines had converted from horsepower to electric cars powered by overhead direct current lines.

Among the numerous trolley companies in Lancaster County were the East End Street Railway and the Lancaster City Street Railway Company. After a number of mergers and acquisitions, all the trolley lines were combined in 1900 to form the Conestoga Traction Company. With one company at the helm, trolley lines began sprawling out to smaller towns throughout the county.

Passengers traveled in open-air cars during warm weather, hopping on board to head to Rocky Springs and Maple Grove for a swim. Suburban lines used large double-truck cars similar to railroad passenger cars. Navigating the city's narrower streets required single-truck cars.

When the Conestoga Traction Company was reorganized in 1931 as the Conestoga Transportation Company, the suburban lines began to be converted to bus lines. Trolley service in Lancaster County ended on September 21, 1947, with the last trip to Rocky Springs Park. A few "Trolley Fan Rambles" were held before the tracks were removed in the winter of 1947.

Left: The Conestoga Traction Company's Car No. 172 awaits passengers at Penn Square, circa 1912. The motorman and conductor posed for the photographer before making a run to Maple Grove. LCHS A-09-01-21.

Above: Two women and a young girl hop aboard a trolley car headed for the Seventh Ward from Penn Square, circa 1918. LCHS 1-01-03-41.

During the 1920s, Lancaster grew and prospered. This view of Penn Square shows the Watt and Shand Building at far right and trolleys surrounding the Soldiers and Sailors Monument. Today the Fulton Bank building would occupy the center background. LCHS 2-05-11-02.

Penn Square, the heart of the city of Lancaster, bustled with trolley traffic when this photo was snapped around 1910. The twin cupolas of the Woolworth Building towered above its rooftop gardens, a popular spot for dancing and entertainment in its day. LCHS 2-07-05-28.

Three Sixth Ward trolleys make their way down North Duke Street, circa 1940. St. James Episcopal Church and its rectory appear in the background. LCHS 2-04-06-02.

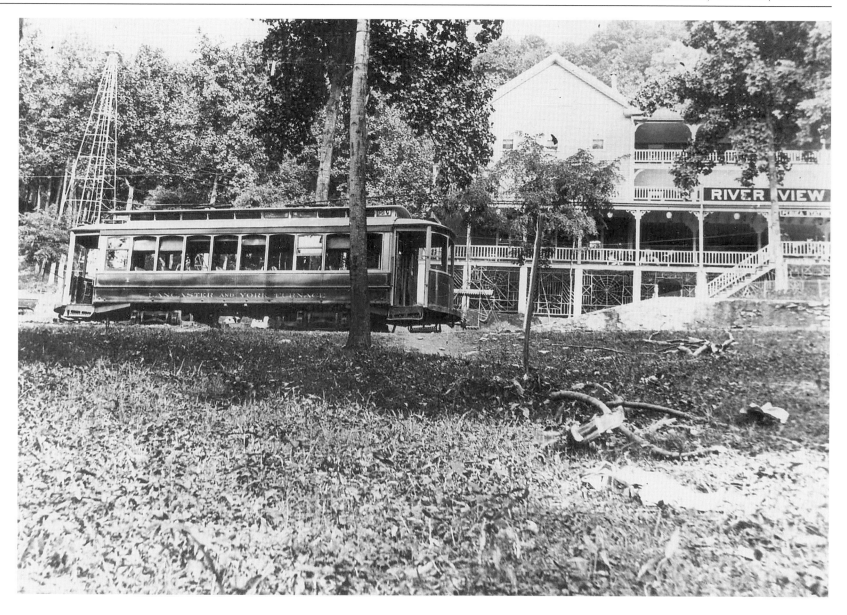

The Lancaster and York Furnace Trolley Car No. 1 passes the River View Hotel near Pequea in southern Lancaster County. The trolley line opened in 1903 to transport passengers to the York Furnace park just south of Pequea. LCHS 1-01-06-09.

The Laurel Street trolley car stops to pick up two passengers at the intersection of South Dorwart and St. Joseph Streets, circa 1943. The Laurel Street and Filbert Street lines, which had previously been taken out of use, were returned to service in the early 1940s. LCHS A-08-01-22.

Left: A crowd gathers to watch workers rebuild the Duke Street bridge over the Pennsylvania Railroad's tracks in the 1930s. The cut under the bridge was filled in after the railroad tracks were removed. Trolley lines were temporarily taken up to help in filling in the space. LCHS 2-04-06-15.

Employees stand in front of the Penn Square to Ephrata trolley as it prepares to make its last run in September of 1947. The lines closed and the tracks were taken up that same winter. LCHS A-09-01-19.

During warm weather, open-air trolleys were put to use to keep passengers cool. The one pictured above is running along College Avenue, north of Columbia Avenue. LCHS 2-07-02-16.

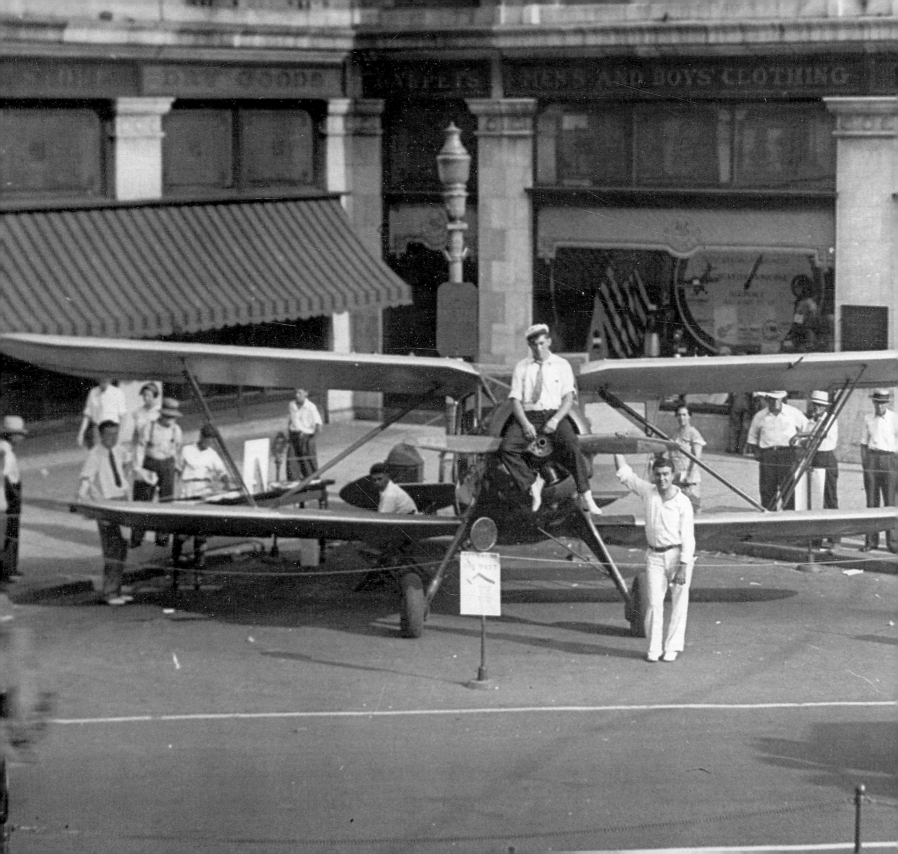

Barnstormers and Grass Strips

William E. Krantz

The 1920s and 1930s have been called the "Golden Age of Aviation." Barnstorming pilots provided thrilling aerial stunt shows, taking off and landing in farmers' open fields. Eventually the barnstormers settled down and started public airports, introducing the public to airplanes as a practical means of transportation. This period saw the transition from open cockpit sport planes to airplanes with enclosed cabins for passenger comfort.

Chambers of commerce were eager to build airports to have their cities ready for the coming age of air travel. Barnstormer Jesse Jones established Lancaster's first airport on leased land along Manheim Pike in 1927, just north of the city limits. In the early 1930s, a citizens' committee selected the present site on Lititz Pike as the permanent location for a municipally owned airfield. The Lancaster Municipal Airport was dedicated in August, 1935.

A few days before that dedication, pilot Art Lamparter and some friends pushed his Waco cabin biplane from the old Manheim Pike airport through the streets to the southeast corner of Penn Square. Hundreds of citizens got a close look at a modern airplane as Lamparter promoted the benefits of air travel.

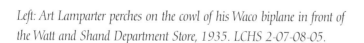

Left: Art Lamparter perches on the cowl of his Waco biplane in front of the Watt and Shand Department Store, 1935. LCHS 2-07-08-05.

Right: Lancaster's premier aviator, Jesse Jones, models a winter flight suit as he stands with a Waco 10 airplane at the old Lancaster airport on Manheim Pike, 1928. LCHS 2-08-05-45.

59

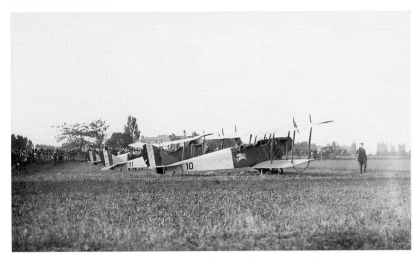

Three U.S. Army airplanes arrived in Lancaster in October, 1918, to promote the sale of Liberty Bonds. Professor Frederic Klein of Franklin & Marshall College described the throngs who gathered at Buchanan Park as a "circus-day crowd. [S]chools, plants and business houses were closed to give everyone a chance to see what was for many their first airplane." The photo at bottom left shows the three Army Air Force pilots who landed their planes in Buchanan Park. Airports did not exist at that time, so pilots landed in any convenient open space. Clockwise from top left: LCHS D-04-04-16, D-04-04-32, D-04-04-24, D-04-04-22.

An air meet at the old Lancaster airport on the Manheim Pike, 1927. The building that now houses CarpetMart served as a hangar at the airfield. LCHS 2-08-05-52.

Biplane at Lancaster airport on Manheim Pike at the Bicentennial Air Meet, July 27 and 28, 1929. The event celebrated Lancaster County's 200th birthday. On the plane's lower wing are the awards contributed by the Bicentennial Committee, Mayor Musser, Chamber of Commerce, Armstrong Cork Company, Follmer Clogg, Hamilton Watch Company, General Tire, Lancaster Newspapers, Watt and Shand, Manufacturers Association, American Business Club, Exchange Club, Kiwanis Club, Lions Club, Rotary Club, Monarch Club, and the Knights of Columbus. An estimated 20,000 spectators attended the Sunday festivities. LCHS D-06-01-19.

Fueling an airplane in the late 1920s at the old Lancaster airport. Five-gallon cans of gasoline from the fuel truck were poured through a chamois filter into the plane's fuel tank. LCHS 2-08-05-47.

Roy K. Geltz operated a flying service at the old Lancaster airport and was a dealer for Piper Cub aircraft. In 1931, he offered flying lessons for $2.50 per lesson. Geltz later developed an airstrip south of Columbia Pike near Donerville. Others used the runway as a drag strip, drawing complaints from the neighbors. LCHS 1-05-01-26.

Ethel Geltz, Roy's wife, in a Stearman airplane at the old Lancaster airport, circa 1946. LCHS 1-05-01-33.

Left: Lancaster Mayor James Ross poses with airport officials and Civil Air Patrol pilots at the airport on Manheim Pike in 1945. Pictured from left to right are Frederic Klein, Roy Geltz, Bruce Boggs, Jessie Jones, Abe Snavely, Mayor Ross, George Ritnour, Helen Jones, Clyde Grissinger, Ben Snavely, and Ed Sterner. During World War II, members of the Civil Air Patrol served as enemy aircraft spotters. LCHS 2-08-02-11.

William F. Slaymaker flies his Fairchild airplane, circa 1932. William Hollowell, chief photographer of the Darmstaetter Photo Supply Co., took the photograph. LCHS 2-08-05-48.

Businessmen involved in promoting Lancaster's airport pose in front of a tri-motor aircraft, circa 1930. The airplane, typical of those used by airlines at the time, flew into the old Lancaster airport on the Manheim Pike. LCHS D-06-01-20.

Pilot Jesse Jones, right, stands with Stuart H. Raub and William S. Raub as they prepare to fly to Wilkes-Barre in February, 1929. The name of the passengers' business, Raub Supply Co., was painted on the fuselage of the Waco 10 airplane. LCHS D-06-01-28.

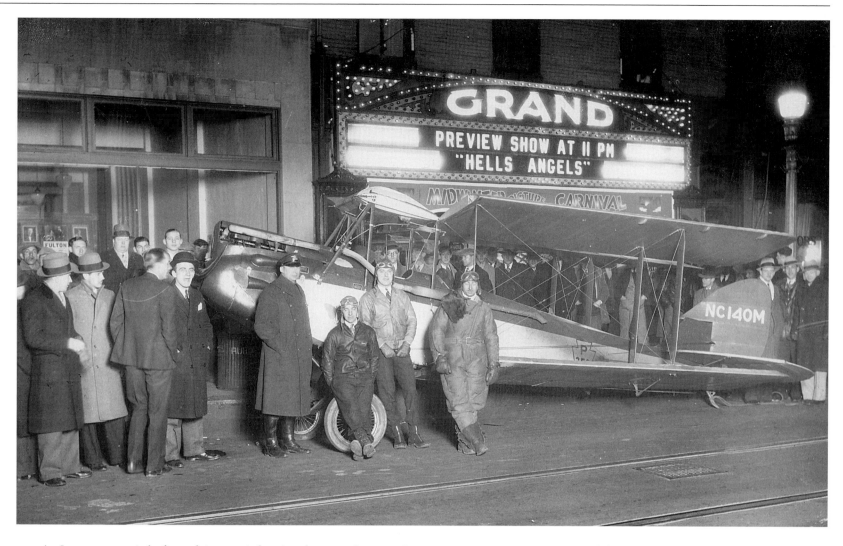

Art Lamparter wasn't the first to bring an airplane into downtown Lancaster. In 1933 airport manager Jesse Jones taxied this Gipsy Moth airplane, with its wings folded back, from the Manheim Pike airport to the Grand Theatre on North Queen Street. The occasion was a preview showing of the movie Hell's Angels. LCHS 2-08-05-50.

Messing About in Boats

Barry R. Rauhauser

Throughout this region's first two centuries of settlement, the Susquehanna River lured many to attempt to create a successful trade route over her unpredictable waters. Lancaster County's inventors confronted the task with varying degrees of success. Hempfield native Daniel Keller patented an ox-powered paddlewheel boat in 1795 and an ark in 1799 in an effort to tame the mighty river. Perhaps also inspired by the Susquehanna, more notable inventors, such as William Henry and Robert Fulton, successfully solved the problem of steam-powered navigation. Although no one ever managed to fully conquer the Susquehanna, the river became the most frequently navigated non-navigable body of water.

While most of us think of boating as a purely recreational pastime, many Lancastrians have relied on boats for an occupation. At times the only way to travel west from Lancaster was via the ferry operations that transported people and products across the river. Attempts at river navigation also resulted in the construction of Pennsylvania's canal system and an influx of arks and canal boats from the northern regions of the state to the towns of Marietta and Columbia. Boats were also used to commercially fish the Susquehanna River. In the twentieth century, large boats dredged tons of waste coal deposits from the river bottom, cleaning up the river while recapturing a valuable energy source.

Living within the nation's largest watershed has influenced more than one Lancastrian to travel by water, whether for business or pleasure. From canoes to powerboats, ferries to arks, rafts to canal boats, many Lancaster citizens have taken to floating on the multitude of waterways in Lancaster County.

Left: A large group, possibly a Union League outing, steps aboard a canal boat for an afternoon excursion, circa 1905. Standing behind the gentleman seated on the railing is Captain Jacob Eby Barr, a noted Civil War veteran from Lancaster. LCHS 3-14-01-07.

Above: The Lady Gay, *Lancaster County's best known steamship. LCHS 2-06-08-11.*

One way to spend a sunny afternoon in 1925 was to float the Conestoga River in a rowboat at Rocky Springs Park. Elmer and Ida Hershey and Ella and Harold Hamilton and an unidentified chap prepare to do just that. LCHS A-09-01-16.

Outing Of Local #95. N.F.P.O.C. Pequea, Pa. August, 14, 1921.

The National Federation of Post Office Clerks Local #95 enjoys a boat ride on the Susquehanna River in 1921. The group visited the Holtwood Power Plant and then had a chicken and waffle dinner at the Pequea Fishing Club. LCHS 2-02-03-10.

An empty Lady Gay paddles beneath the trolley bridge and stone arches of Witmer's Bridge, just below Lancaster on the Conestoga River, circa 1900. The Lady Gay plied the Conestoga from Witmer's Bridge to Rocky Springs Park from the 1890s to 1915. LCHS 2-06-08-12.

The Lady Gay, along with her sister ships, the Evelyn B. and the Nellie B., was piloted along the Conestoga River by Capt. John Peoples. LCHS 2-06-08-14.

During the Lady Gay's heyday, it was quite popular for gentlemen to take their lady friends out for a romantic sail on the Conestoga to Rocky Springs Park. Captain Peoples also piloted folks to his own Peoples Bathing Resort. LCHS 2-06-08-10.

During the summer months, canoes and rowboats were available for visitors to Rocky Springs Park, a popular bathing resort and amusement park. A float on the river was a sure way to cool off on a hot day. LCHS 2-06-08-05.

Passengers board the Steamboat Mary for a jaunt on the Susquehanna River between Columbia and Wrightsville, circa 1900. LCHS 2-06-08-13.

Everyone in Lancaster knew Darmstaetter's as a photo supply house, but the store also sold boats. In 1931 their second floor display included canoes, rowboats, and small motorized seagoing craft. LCHS D-10-04-20.

Douglas Darmstaetter, left, and his brother Harcourt show off a boat to two lovely young ladies, circa 1955. LCHS D-10-03-76.

The Horseless Carriage

Tamsin Wolff

At the turn of the twentieth century, the world of the "horse and buggy" was at the crossroads of a new era. Bicycle and carriage makers, metalworkers, and machinists were trying to become auto manufacturers. It was a time of experimentation, with no standardized parts and inefficient production methods.

In 1903, the Safety Buggy Works, located at Elizabeth Avenue and North Plum Street in Lancaster, became the first company in the county to build an automobile. Safety Buggy Works operated from about 1897 to 1908. Byron G. Dodge owned the company. His son Leon Dodge ran it.

Milton Hershey was among the first Lancastrians to buy an automobile. He bought the car at the New York Auto Show—a floor model of a Riker Electric, which he purchased for $2,000, pricey for its day. The car was the first of its kind in Pennsylvania. It was equipped with electric lights, an electric bell, and a top speed of nine miles per hour. Hershey toured the state in the car, selling candies to the crowds that gathered to see it.

Although the 1900 curved dash Oldsmobile was America's first mass-produced car, it wasn't until Henry Ford introduced the *continued…*

Left: Cars and trucks wait in line to cross railroad tracks in Columbia, circa 1925. Among the vehicles that can be identified are a Buick (center) and a Metropolitan Edison company truck. LCHS D-06-01-36.

Above: A car in the Ford/Lincoln showroom at Garden Spot Motor Company, 450 North Prince Street, Lancaster, circa 1929. LCHS D-06-03-32.

81

Model T in 1908 that millions of Americans could purchase one—for only $850. Former bicycle salesman Samuel Roth was the first to be listed in the Lancaster City Directory as an auto dealer in 1903. Among the models he sold were the Duryea, the Rambler Alco, and the Haynes-Apperson. He also repaired cars and was well known to many of the prominent early auto innovators, including Henry Ford, Thomas Edison, and Harvey Firestone. Edison apparently visited Roth in Lancaster on one occasion, having driven here in his White Steamer. Roth closed his garage during World War I because most of his mechanics were called into military service. He never went back to selling or working on cars, instead opening a grocery store and gas station on Harrisburg Avenue.

Mechanics at the auto repair shop of James G. Robbins work on a fleet of Ramblers, circa 1910. Pictured from right are Jim Robbins, Horace Zecher, and two unidentified employees. The shop was located at 112–116 South Water Street in Lancaster. LCHS 2-03-06-24.

Leon Dodge, manager of the Safety Buggy Works, along with his brother, Arthur, stand around one of the first automobiles built in Lancaster County. This photo, taken in 1903, includes Horace and Charles E. Zecher, employees in the smith department. LCHS 2-06-03-10.

Photographed circa 1912, this Pierce-Arrow touring car appears ready for a drive through the Lancaster County countryside. LCHS D-06-01-42.

An elderly couple sits for a picture in front of a large touring car, circa 1910. LCHS A-10-01-01.

Three dapper fellows prepare for a ride in their touring car, possibly a 1922 Haynes. LCHS D-06-03-87.

Anthony L. Steckel of Pleasure Road in Lancaster prepares for a road trip, 1928. LCHS D-06-01-46.

A young couple heads out for a drive on a rural road in their 1922 Ford Speedster. Note the hand crank hanging over the license plate. Starting cars in the 1920s wasn't as easy as turning a key. LCHS D-06-01-59.

A Gardner motor car fuels up at the Traylor Motor Garage at 114 South Queen Street during a 1924 endurance run. Cannonball Baker, whose name appears on the car, was one of the most popular auto racers of the time. LCHS D-06-01-68.

Not long after the invention of the automobile came the invention of the automobile race. As soon as someone figured out how to put an engine on wheels, it seemed almost necessary to find out how fast it would go and how far it would run. Endurance runs were quite the fad in the early part of the twentieth century, with some drivers gaining celebrity status. Erwin Baker earned himself the nickname "Cannonball" for his speedy coast-to-coast travels.

Jack Davis, another auto enthusiast, planned to set off from Lancaster for a 100-hour endurance run on July 8, 1930. C. Eugene Longenecker, proprietor of a Lancaster garage and automobile dealership, provided Davis with a brand new DeSoto Straight 8 for the occasion. The run hit a pothole when Longenecker and Davis were arrested on July 10. Failing to heed a warning from the local police, the pair were brought in by Corporal Harry Myers of the Pennsylvania State Highway Patrol. While many looked at these races as fun on wheels, the authorities considered them reckless driving.

Endurance runs also served as good advertising for early motor car companies. The latest models of Franklins, Gardners, and Haynes all sped through Lancaster County on promotional jaunts.

Top right: Police officers talk with driver Jack Davis at the beginning of a 100-hour endurance run in 1930. Local dealer C. Eugene Longenecker, son of J. F. Longenecker, provided the car. Davis and Longenecker were later arrested on charges of reckless driving. LCHS D-06-05-36.

Right: An air-cooled Franklin, with its distinctive "vacuum cleaner" front end, departs for a short endurance run from Lancaster to Philadelphia and back in 1920. Endurance runs often promoted new automobile models. LCHS D-06-01-75.

This little coupe, possibly a Mercedes, was photographed for the Schutte Body Company in 1922. The company built car bodies, primarily for Dusenberg and Oldsmobile, from 1918 to 1927. Charles E. Schutte, the son of a carriage maker, operated his business on South West End Avenue. LCHS 1-02-04-02.

A man and his two children pose with their new car—a Marmon, perhaps—in front of the Whallon Tobacco Company in 1928. Notice the family dog behind the steering wheel. LCHS D-06-01-52.

Alderman John F. Burkhart takes his Stutz 8 for a spin on Buchanan Avenue during the winter of 1928. LCHS D-06-01-55.

Right: Father, daughter, and puppy prepare to set out for a ride in their Buick touring car, circa 1910. LCHS D-06-01-62.

Dr. Theodore Gabel, a Lancaster dentist, and a female companion go for a drive in his Buick, circa 1918. LCSH D-06-01-64.

Guy S. Burkholder Chrysler shows off the 1926 Chrysler Victoria Coupe in front of their showroom, 59 North Duke Street, in Lancaster. LCHS D-06-03-47.

A banged-up late 1920s Buick awaits repairs at a local Gulf station. The mismatched hubcaps and the wear on the tires (including the spare) suggest that this car had been around the block more than once. LCHS D-06-02-04.

An unattended 1947 Chevy drifted into a precarious position along McGovern Avenue in 1954. Onlookers tried to figure out how to dislodge the car. LCHS 1-02-03-69.

The new fleet of 1935 Packards is displayed in style at North Prince Street Motors, 426 North Prince Street, in Lancaster. Early car dealerships were more floral than modern ones. LCHS D-06-03-24.

In 1930, the latest Fords could be found at the Hatton Wolf Motor Company. Its showroom was located at 1022 North Prince Street in Lancaster. LCHS D-06-03-28.

Fill 'Er Up!

Tamsin Wolff

At the turn of the twentieth century drivers purchased gasoline in cans from bicycle shops, hardware stores, or livery depots. Filling up a horseless carriage was a messy three-person job, requiring a large funnel, a makeshift filter made of chamois, and a metal canister filled with gasoline. A wooden dipstick with graduated markings served as a fuel gauge.

Flory Brothers Motorcycle and Supply Company typified the many businesses that added gasoline to their inventories. About 1910, forward-thinking stores installed dedicated curbside gas pumps, signaling that they were friendly to motorists. Early pumps were hand cranked. A dial with numbers let consumers know how much gas they had pumped. It took about eight minutes to fill a five-gallon tank.

Growing oil refineries began to advertise and create a brand image. Signs and slogans called out to customers from every conceivable street position.

continued…

Above: A busy day for the mechanics at Eli B. Powl's garage at 16 East Walnut Street, Lancaster, in 1924. LCHS D-06-05-06.

Left: The Atlantic Gasoline service station at the junction of Orange and King Streets in Lancaster welcomes drivers entering the city's west end in 1927. LCHS D-06-04-20.

By the 1920s it became common to see a large porcelain enameled sign raised high on a pole or attached to a station. Glowing tubes of neon debuted in 1923.

Gas stations developed a unique architecture and were the first commercial buildings to be set back from the street to accommodate automobiles. The first dedicated "drive-up" service station opened in Pittsburgh in 1913. Adapted barn structures were slowly replaced by company stations, with separate pump islands and a unified design. They varied in style from Greek temples and Japanese shrines to office- and homelike structures. Service "palaces" and ornate "lubritoriums" evolved with pagoda roofs, cupolas, night lighting, and slogans advertising "that good gasoline."

By 1935 Americans were pumping more than 15 billion gallons of gas annually at over 200,000 stations. Up to the 1970s, "gas jockeys" in starched shirts and lab coats greeted customers, pumped gas, wiped the windshield, measured the oil, and checked tire pressure. Soiled uniforms or greasy rags hanging from pockets were not to be seen. In the service bays, mechanics labored out of sight in the "pits," work areas recessed into the floor, which provided access to the car's underside.

The signpost at John R. Henney's Atlantic station on Harrisburg Pike advertised everything from coal and electric furnaces to chicken and waffles, 1929.
LCHS D-06-04-14.

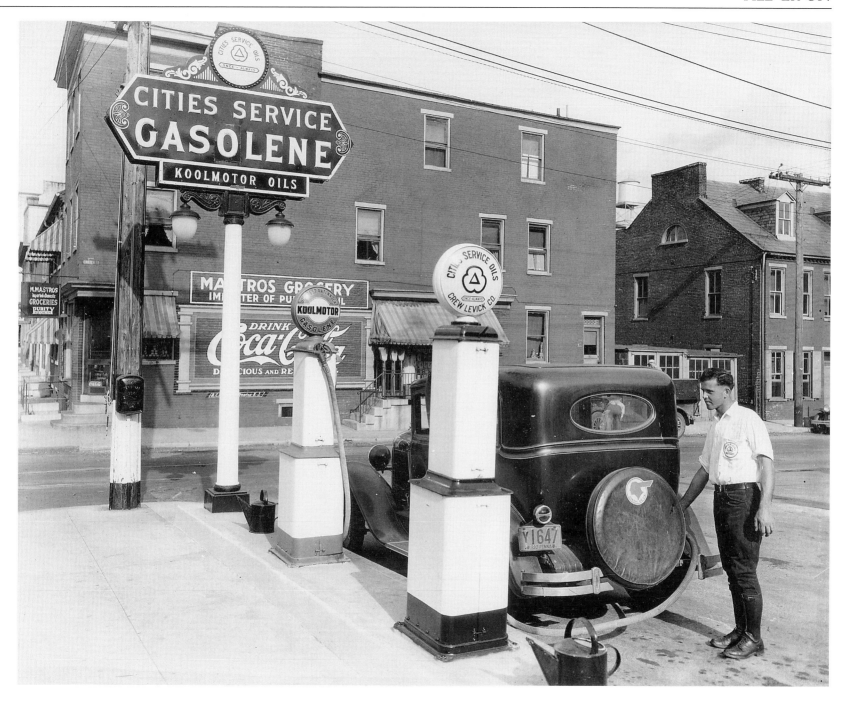

In 1930, drivers could fill up their tanks at Cities Service Gasolene at Orange and Water Streets and get a soda across the street at the Mastros Grocery store. LCHS D-06-04-24.

Located at the junction of Marietta and Orange Streets, the General Tire Company advertised "tires, tubes and repairs, special road equipment for handling giant pneumatics and solid tires" in Polk's Lancaster City Directory for 1930, the year this photo was taken. LCHS D-06-04-31.

At Jacob and Daniel Flory's cycle and supply shop at 161 East King Street, a gentleman fills up his Franklin's tank, circa 1917. Early gas stations didn't always have an outside pump. At Flory Brothers, the gas hose ran to a pump inside or behind the shop. LCHS D-06-04-32a.

Charles S. Hoffman and Ernest H. Miller sold and serviced Pierce-Arrow automobiles at their establishment at 1423 East King Street near Bridgeport, as shown in this circa 1927 photograph. LCHS D-06-04-46.

In 1926, the Stehman Brothers not only serviced and painted automobiles, but sold Fords as well. Their business served Salunga for many years. LCHS D-06-04-63.

By 1930, the garage had moved out of the backyard barn and become a full service business. At Ed Stumpf's Filling Station at the intersection of the Manheim and Fruitville Pikes, drivers could fill up their tanks and get a tune-up. LCHS D-06-04-67.

A mechanic at the Garden Spot Motor Company on North Prince Street works on a Ford Model T elevated on a lift, circa 1931. LCHS D-06-04-76.

This wasn't just the part of the garage where they changed the oil. This was the Lubritorium of the General Tire Company at 625 West Orange Street, circa 1931. LCHS D-06-04-80.

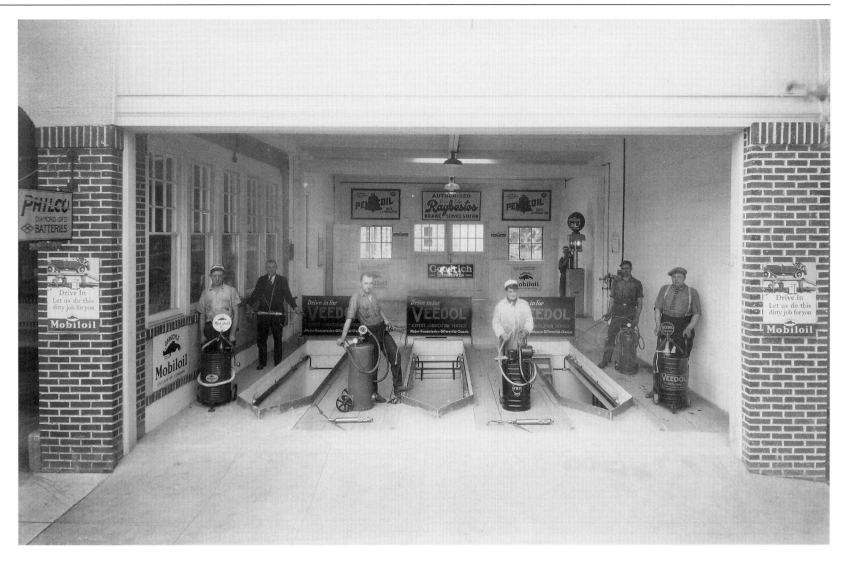

The mechanics at Stumpf's Garage take a break to pose for a picture, 1926. LCHS D-06-04-97.

Harry C. Huber sold and repaired autos at his garage near Lampeter. Note the Ford sign on the building to the right. The photograph was taken in 1920. LCHS D-06-05-05.

The mechanic's white lab coat gives a clinical appearance to Garagit, Inc., in 1930. Garagit was located at North Queen Street and McGovern Avenue in Lancaster, a short distance from the new Pennsylvania Railroad station. LCHS D-06-04-85.

Billboards on Wheels

Marianne Heckles

While trains could haul freight long distances, the commercial vehicle—the trusted truck—was perfect for local deliveries. Trucks picked up where the horse and wagon left off, hauling anything from furniture to groceries to fuel oil and coal.

As businesses grew, it became apparent that commercial vehicles were not just a means of transportation. They could also serve as a form of advertising. A catchy logo or design on the side of a truck seen tooling around town could lure in intrigued customers. Some companies simply painted their name and address on their trucks, maybe with a trademarked insignia. Others saw the truck as a billboard, using the whole vehicle to its fullest advantage.

Lancaster's Heidelbaugh Coal Company was known far and wide for its fleet of checkered coal and fuel oil trucks. Going one step further was the Keystone Furniture Company. It operated in the first block of West King Street in Lancaster during the 1920s and 1930s. To celebrate the company's fourteenth anniversary, owner Miles Goodman had a "House on Wheels" built and drove it around the city to drum up business.

Advertising and trucking have evolved considerably in the intervening years. But whether moving your furniture, towing your car, or catching your eye, trucks remain the reliable workhorse of most businesses.

Left: A busy day for Arthur L. Youart's hauling company, circa 1927. Piled high with furniture, his REO Speed Wagon is pictured here on the 300 block of North Queen Street next to James F. Wild's auto parts store. LCHS D-06-02-61.

Above: H. K. Dorsheimer's Wholesale Confectionery delivered its products in a Dodge truck in 1925. LCHS D-06-02-38.

In 1922, Hamilton Watch's company vehicle was a shiny Dodge Brothers truck. LCHS D-06-02-77.

The Conestoga and Lancaster Auto Bus, 1929. Earl Myers delivered passengers and mail in the Lancaster and Millersville areas during the 1920s. LCHS D-06-02-88.

Auto owners needing roadside assistance in 1930 could count on Frank M. Abel's Firestone Service Station on Wheels. Firestone's non-mobile service station was located at 111 West Chestnut Street in Lancaster. LCHS D-06-02-57.

A Christian Kunzler Company delivery truck with James H. Waltz behind the wheel, 1928. Waltz worked as a route salesman for many years before retiring in 1961. LCHS D-06-03-04.

The Keystone Furniture Company, a fixture on West King Street in the 1920s and 1930s, delivered sofas and chairs right to the customer's door. This truck was in service in 1929. LCHS D-06-02-92.

Keystone Furniture had a less functional vehicle built in 1928 to celebrate the company's fourteenth anniversary. The "House on Wheels" must have been quite a sight driving around Lancaster. LCHS D-06-03-05.

Justus B. Wiggins delivered groceries in his Dodge Brothers truck in 1926. He operated his store at the corner of West Lemon and Nevin Streets until his death in 1958. LCHS D-06-03-18.

Tourists aboard the Garden Spot Sight-Seeing Parlor Car in 1926 came to Lancaster County to experience the same beautiful landscapes modern visitors do. LCHS D-06-03-14.

With watermelons and baseball bats in tow, the newsboys of the Meekins News Agency head off for a picnic in the summer of 1920. LCHS D-11-05-08.

Keppel Brothers' General Motors truck delivers candy that puts "Pep in Your Step" to the Pennsylvania Railroad station in Lancaster, circa 1925. The wholesale and manufacturing business operated under several incarnations at 323 North Queen Street from 1918 to 1987. LCHS D-06-03-31.

Harry R. Mehaffey operated this tow truck in 1929. Mehaffey was also the proprietor of the Empire Garage and Truck Service, located near Harrisburg Pike and Race Avenue in Lancaster. LCHS D-06-03-01.

The tow truck of Roy Boohar and Ellwood Harnish hauls a wrecked sedan back to their garage at Engleside, circa 1931. LCHS D-06-01-99.

If a little advertising goes a long way, then a fleet of distinctive trucks should drive your business into first place. Perhaps that was the theory behind William Heidelbaugh's checkerboard trucks. His trademark vehicles spurred the business's heyday in the 1920s.

Heidelbaugh co-founded Heidelbaugh Coal Company with William Shand in 1919. As a past president of the now defunct Advertisers' Club, he knew that if the checkered trucks didn't catch the customer's eye, painting the buildings and fences of his business might work. A slightly checkerboard landscape emerged at his coal yards near North Marshall Street.

A fair businessman, Heidelbaugh provided off-season work for his employees. They built more than a hundred homes along Lehigh Avenue and New Holland Avenue east of Franklin Street in Lancaster. The company continued under Heidelbaugh's leadership until 1932 when he sold it to Ralph Coho, and it became the Peoples' Coal Company.

William Heidelbaugh died in 1959, but the images of his checkerboard trucks still linger in the minds of many a Lancastrian.

Left: Heidelbaugh's checkerboard design eventually spread to the buildings in the coal yard. LCHS D-06-02-52.

Above: Two of the company's Mack trucks pose in front of a heap of coal, circa 1931. LCHS D-06-02-70.

Contributors

MARIANNE HECKLES is a graduate of Kutztown University. She is a research assistant and coordinator of photograph collections of the Lancaster County Historical Society.

WILLIAM E. KRANTZ is a retired Lancaster businessman and a graduate of Franklin & Marshall College. He is a past president of the Lancaster Aero Club and a member of the Publications Committee of the Lancaster County Historical Society.

JOHN WARD WILLSON LOOSE is editor-in-chief of the *Journal of the Lancaster County Historical Society* as well as a Fellow of the Lancaster County Historical Society (FLCHS). He graduated from Millersville State Teachers College, now Millersville University, and taught for many years in the Donegal School District

BARRY R. RAUHAUSER is the Stauffer Curator at the Lancaster County Historical Society. He graduated with a B.A. from Penn State University and an M.A. from the University of Delaware's Winterthur Program in Early American Culture.

THOMAS R. RYAN, Ph.D., is the executive director of the Lancaster County Historical Society. He has a master's degree from the Winterthur Program in Early American Culture as well as a doctorate in American Civilization from the University of Delaware. He has taught at Franklin & Marshall College and Millersville University.

THOMAS R. WINPENNY, Ph.D., is a history professor at Elizabethtown College. He served as a trustee of the Lancaster County Historical Society for twenty years and is a member of the historical society's Publications Committee. He has written numerous books and articles about Lancaster County's industrial history.

TAMSIN WOLFF is the director of education at the Antique Automobile Club of America Museum in Hershey, Pennsylvania, where she develops interdisciplinary programs and educational materials for all age groups. She has a master's degree in Museum Education from George Washington University and has worked in art, history, and natural history museums in the mid-Atlantic region for twenty years. She thanks PAUL HERR, an indispensable volunteer, for his assistance. An engineer for 30 years with NASA and New Holland Mechanics, Mr. Herr's lifelong interest in automobiles dates back to age eight, when he disassembled a Ford Model T.

Index

(* indicates illustration)